TROUT Fever

CARTOONS FROM THE LIAR'S LAIR

by Bruce Cochran

Willow Creek Press

Copyright ©1993 by Bruce Cochran

Published by
Willow Creek Press
An imprint of NorthWord Press, Inc.
Box 1360, Minocqua, WI 54548

ISBN 1-55971-148-5

For information on other Willow Creek titles, or for a free color catalog describing NorthWords's line of nature books and gifts, write or call 1-800-336-5666.

Designed by Russell S. Kuepper
Printed in the U.S.A.

All rights reserved. No part of this book may be reproduced or transmitted in any form or by any means, electronic or mechanical, including photocopying, recording or copying by any information storage and retrieval system, without permission in writing from the publisher, except by a reviewer who wishes to include up to three cartoons in connection with a review to include title, author, publisher, publisher's address and price of book, written for inclusion in a magazine or newspaper.

Library of Congress Cataloging-in-Publication Data

Cochran, Bruce.
    Trout fever : cartoons from the liar's lair / by Bruce Cochran.
    p.   cm.
    ISBN 1-55971-148-5. -- ISBN 1-55971-149-3 : $7.95
    1. Fly fishing--Caricatures and cartoons. 2. American wit and humor , Pictorial.   I. Title
NC1429.C619A4   1993
741.5'973--dc20   92-43803
                                                         CIP

For Doc

ABOUT THE FEVERED MIND
OF BRUCE COCHRAN

Cartoonist Bruce Cochran brings his humor to us from a broad background in the outdoors as well as the arts.

Graduating from Oklahoma University with his Bachelor's in Design, he worked for Hallmark Cards as a writer/illustrator, and soon moved on to freelancing jobs with such publications as *Playboy, Look, Saturday Evening Post, Sports Afield, Field & Stream,* and the nation's #1 selling newspaper, *USA Today.* His previous cartoon collections for Willow Creek Press include *Buck Fever, Bass Fever* and *Duck Fever.*

His interest in the outdoors makes Cochran an avid hunter, fisherman, and collector of antique duck decoys. A sponsor member of Ducks Unlimited, his watercolors have been exhibited at the Easton, MD, Waterfowl Festival and the National Ducks Unlimited Wildlife Art Show, among others.

Cochran is married to his wife of 34 years, has two children and has, he says, "been trained by a succession of three Labrador retrievers."

"I don't know, Larry . . . this year I feel like, somewhere, there's a #14 Adams with my name on it."

"Bottom row: Size 24: Black Gnat, Blue-Winged Olive, Elk Hair Caddis, Hendrickson, and . . . uh . . . that's either an Adams or a Light Cahill."

"EAT IT?! Are you kidding?? I'm having this baby MOUNTED!!"

I HAVE TO LEARN THE LATIN NAMES OF TWENTY INSECTS BY TOMORROW.
FOR BIOLOGY CLASS?
NO! FOR FLY FISHING!
COCHRAN!

PERRIER BOTTLES...
...CAVIAR CONTAINERS!
SOMETIMES I WISH YUPPIES HAD NEVER TAKEN UP FLY FISHING!
COCHRAN!

"I don't want to make a fashion statement. I just want some fishing clothes."

"I don't know if these flys catch fish but they definitely catch FISHERMEN."

"Remember those glasses that guy dropped in the river last week? You wouldn't believe how well I can see out of the water with them."

"Sell me something! ANYTHING! I just found an empty pocket in my fishing vest!"

"I found that hole you were talking about."

"What are you using?"

"If I'm supposed to hold my rod at twelve o'clock what do I do between now and twelve?"

"Things may have changed a little since the last time I fished this place."

"It's not just a rod and reel, sir! It's a 'nymph presentation system'."

NEOPRENE

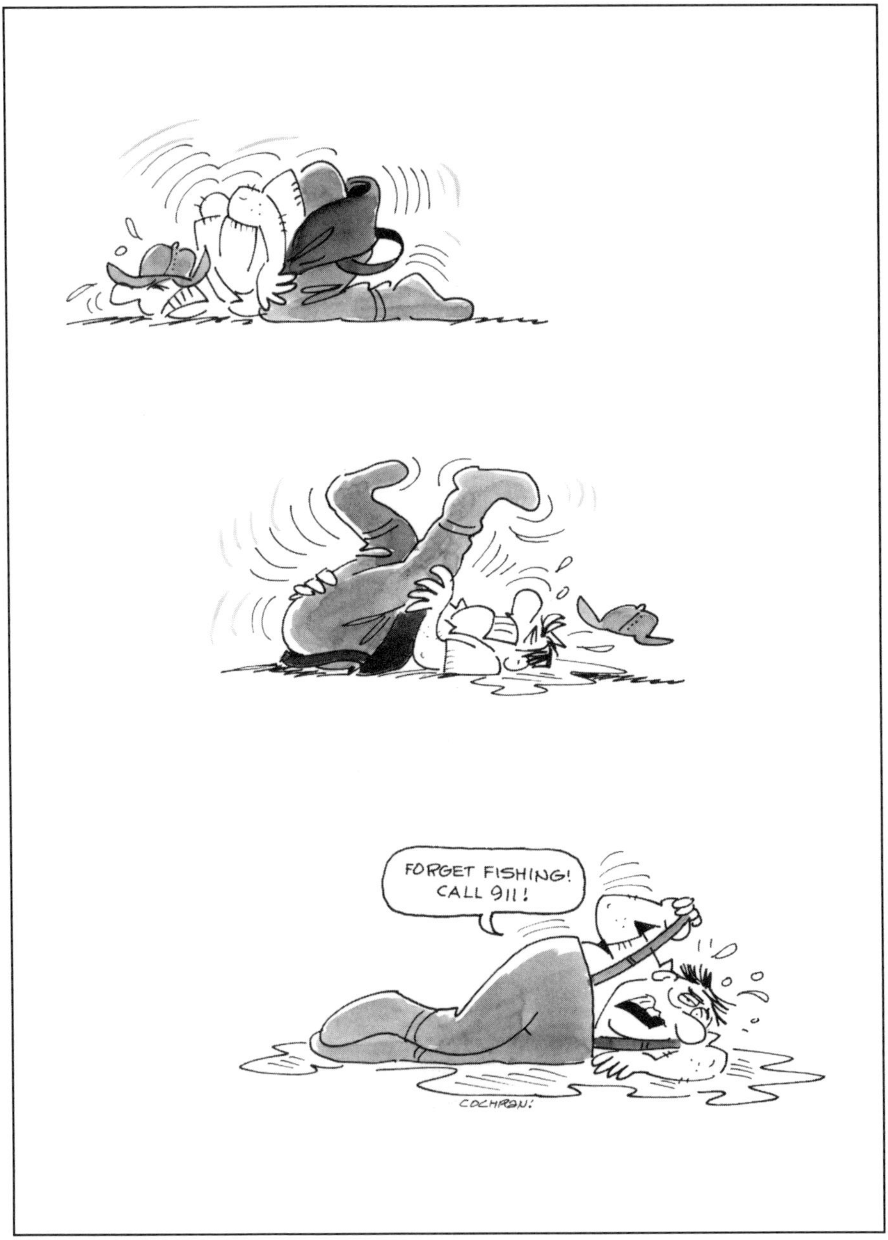
FORGET FISHING!
CALL 911!
COCHRAN!

ASK ABOUT OUR FLY FISHING STARTER KIT
LET'S START WITH THIS 8½, 5-WEIGHT ROD...
... AND OF COURSE YOU'LL NEED A REEL WITH DOUBLE TAPER LINE AND EXTRA SPOOLS FOR WEIGHT-FORWARD AND SINKING LINES...
... AND THIS 75 POCKET VEST FOR FLYS, STREAM THERMOMETER, LEADERS, FLASHLIGHT AND OTHER ACCESSORIES...

...AND FORM-FITTING NEOPRENE WADERS, DESIGNED BY SOME GUY IN MONTANA, IN YOUR CHOICE OF SEVEN DESIGNER COLORS...
...AND... HEY! WHERE ARE YOU GOING?
COCHRAN!

"HONEST! I didn't know about your nest! I'll fish somewhere else . . . no problem . . . "

"We seen you out here in that life raft, mister. Your ship sink or somethin'?"

"I finally found a fly-tying book I like."

"Felt soles."

TROUT FISHING MEETS THE BLUES

"I'D RATHER FISH MUDDY WATER... HANG UP ON A HOLLOW LOG..."

MAY I HAVE A LOCK OF YOUR HAIR?
HOW ROMANTIC! TO CARRY IN YOUR WALLET?
NO. FOR FLY TYING.
COCHRAN!

"I'm not hitting right now, but if I WAS hitting I wouldn't hit THAT."

"Take me to your leader . . . preferably a nine foot knotless taper with a 6x Tippet."

"Whaddaya mean I have a narrow range of interests?! I like to catch rainbows, browns, cutthroats . . ."

"What're they hittin' on?"

"I'll be glad when something to EAT comes along. All we've seen all day are these damn furwing floozies!"

"Tonight on 'Crossfire:' Is using a strike indicator REALLY fly fishing? On the right, Carl Richards. On the left, Lefty Kreh . . ."

"It's a plastic replica of the guy who caught and released me."

LIFE CYCLE OF THE MAYFLY

NYMPH

EMERGER

DUN

LUNCH

"This fly calls for hare's ear and I don't have a hare . . . hmmmmm . . . but, hey! I DO have a dog!"

"I tied it especially for Uncle Charlie. It's an artificial marshmallow."

"Just because it's not an ant, a beetle, or a grasshopper doesn't mean it's not a terrestrial."

"You can't imagine what it's like to be owned by a fly-tyer."

"I had just finished tying two dozen size 22 light cahills (sob). Then I SNEEZED!"

DON'T FORGET FLY TYING RULE NUMBER 32.
WHAT'S THAT?
THE FLY YOU TIE A DOZEN OF TONIGHT IS NEVER THE ONE THEY WANT TOMORROW.
COCHRAN!

FLY-TYING GROUPIES
WATCHING YOU TIE IN THAT HACKLE GAVE ME GOOSE BUMPS!
I LOVE A MAN WHO SMELLS LIKE HEAD CEMENT!
I'LL BET YOU CAN DO SOME REALLY KINKY THINGS WITH THESE FEATHERS!
COCHRAN

"Can't you sing anything besides 'Over the Rainbow'?"

"Hand me a weight-forward sinking tip six-weight line with a nine foot knotless 5x leader and a #18 isonychia nymph."

"Don't you just hate it when you think you're taking a big bite of *Stenomena canadense* and it turns out to be a Light Cahill?"

"She's cute, but she's got no personality."

"Maybe you'd better forget the triple-haul backhand slack-line power cast and just try to get your fly in the water."

WHAT ARE YOU USING?
A #18 ADAMS.
ON A 7½', 5X TAPERED LEADER...
WITH 18" OF 6X TIPPET...

WITH A 4-WEIGHT DOUBLE TAPER FLOATING LINE...
AND AN 8' GRAPHITE ROD WITH A DISK DRAG ALUMINUM ALLOY REEL...
ASK SOME PEOPLE WHAT TIME IT IS AND THEY'LL TELL YOU HOW TO MAKE A WATCH.
COCHRAN!

THE
EVENING HATCH
IS BROUGHT TO YOU BY
LARRY'S FLY SHOP
RODS • REELS • LINES
FLY TYING MATERIALS
COCHRAN!

"It's my 'Uncle Charlie Survival Kit.' Antacids, bug repellent, and room deodorizer."

"Uncle Charlie practices catch-and-release woman chasing."

"I've caught bullheads, gar, and drum, kid. All I need now is a carp to complete my grand slam."

"Good news and bad news, kid. The bad news is, the dog ate our bait. The good news is, we can get it back tomorrow."

SPECIAL
RED NECK REGULATIONS
AREA
CORN, CHEESE, SALMON EGGS,
WORMS, MARSHMALLOWS ONLY!
ALL TROUT CAUGHT MUST BE KEPT
ON A BIG RUSTY METAL STRINGER.
COCHRAN!

YOU'LL NEVER BELIEVE THIS LITTLE STREAM I'M TAKIN' US TO!
IT'S FULL OF CUTTHROATS AS LONG AS YOUR LEG...

... AND YOU CAN ONLY GET THERE BY 4-WHEEL DRIVE!
OR HORSEBACK.
COCHRAN!

I'VE SEEN THE MADISON SO THICK WITH RAINBOWS YOU COULD WALK ACROSS IT ON THEIR BACKS!
I'VE CAUGHT TROUT IN THE FIREHOLE, BOILED 'EM IN A HOT SPRING, AND EATEN 'EM RIGHT THERE IN THE RIVER!
I'VE CAUGHT SO MANY BROOKIES IN THE LETORT THEY HAD TO RESTOCK IT AFTER I LEFT!

I'VE CAUGHT BROWNS IN THE AUSABLE AS LONG AS YOUR LEG!
I'VE STOOD KNEE-DEEP IN THE BIG HORN AND CAUGHT CUTTHROATS 'TIL MY ARMS ACHED!
WE'RE KNEE-DEEP IN SOMETHING RIGHT NOW BUT IT'S SURE AS HELL NOT THE BIG HORN.
COCHRAN!

THINK I'LL PUT ON A #18 PARACHUTE ADAMS.
THINK I'LL PUT ON A # 20 FAN WING ROYAL COACHMAN.
THINK I'LL PUT ON A #6 TREBLE HOOK WITH A BIG BLOB OF VELVEETA.
COCHRAN

"Here, kid. Take these pancakes over to the table. And don't drop any!
The dog will roll in 'em and they'll take his hair off!"

"My teacher says when we kid Uncle Charlie about fishing with worms we're guilty of baitism."

YOU'LL LIKE THESE TROUT. I SMOKED 'EM MYSELF!
HICKORY?
MESQUITE?
CIGAR!
COCHRAN!

"For 15-20 pancakes mix 2 cups of milk . . .

. . . one and a half cups of mix . . .

. . . and two eggs."

"I don't really have to go, kid! I'm just markin' my territory."

"Don't dump those worms, kid! I'm makin' chili tonight!"

"Uncle Charlie, have you seen my boom box?"

"What's the matter, kid? You never heard of trout chili before?"

"The secret is to get your WD-40 good and hot, then roll your fish in good fresh kitty litter . . ."

"Eat your heart out, Julia Child!"

"Why the hell do we have fried potatoes left? I only cooked five pounds per person!"

"UNCLE CHARLIE! THERE'S A COCKROACH ON THE TABLE!"

"PUT HIM BACK IN THE CHILI WHERE HE BELONGS."

"I've heard of pancakes sticking to the SKILLET. But never to the ceiling."

YOU WOULDN'T BELIEVE THE TROUT I CAUGHT LAST FALL!...
WHEN I SET THE HOOK HE RAN OFF ABOUT TWO MILES OF LINE!
LUCKY FOR ME THE ROAD RUNS RIGHT ALONG THE RIVER, SO I FLAGGED DOWN A BEER TRUCK AND FOLLOWED HIM!

WHEN HE REACHED THE OLD BRIDGE PILINGS HE DOVE FOR THE BOTTOM! I KNEW I COULDN'T HORSE HIM IN...
...SO I TIED MY POLE TO A TREE AND WALKED HOME TO GET A SADDLE! I WAS GONNA DIVE IN, SADDLE HIM UP, AND RIDE HIM INTO TOWN AND SHOW HIM OFF...
...BUT WHEN I GOT BACK THE SUMBITCH HAD UPROOTED THE TREE AND TAKEN OFF!
COCHRAN!

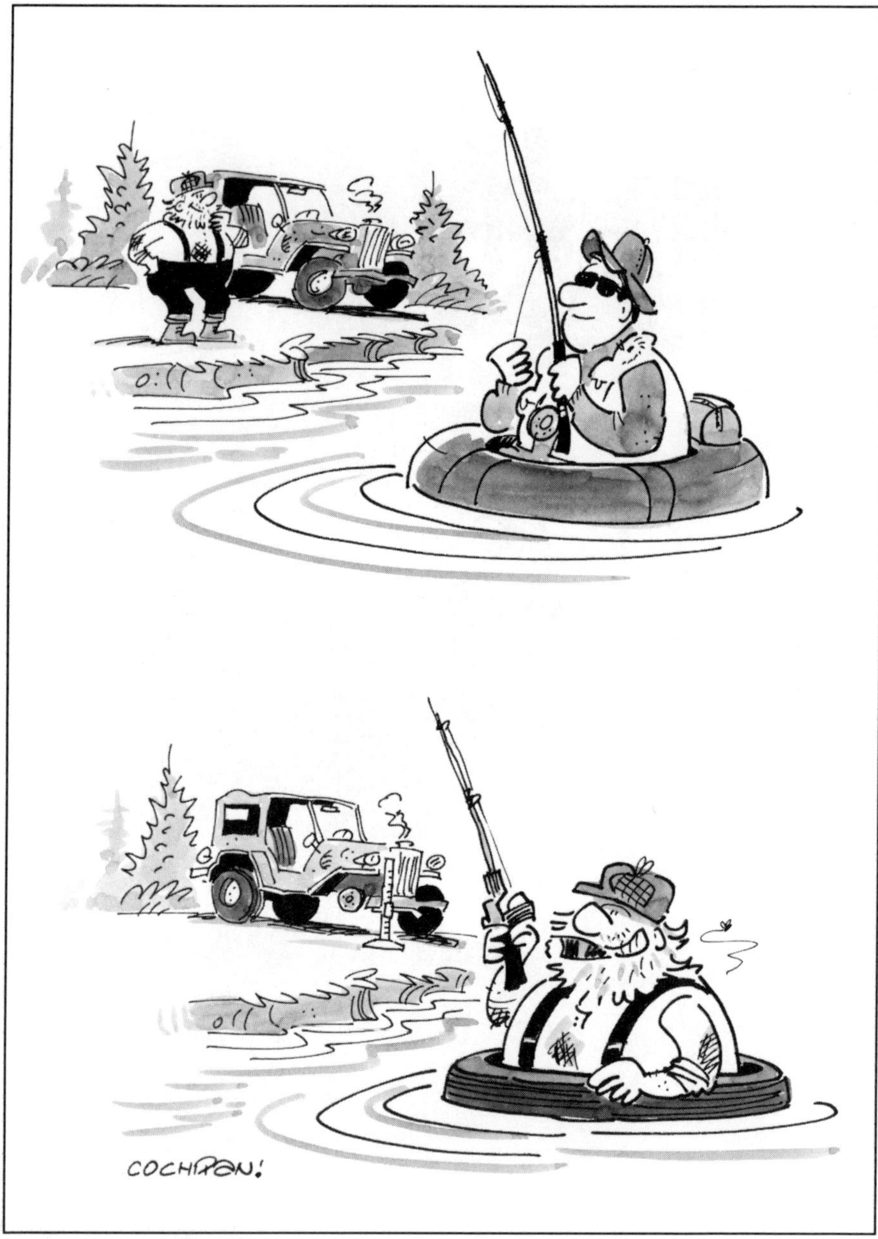
COCHRAN!

"I've got an egg and some worms . . . Hey! I can make an omelette!"

UNCLE CHARLIE AND I WENT NIGHT FISHING FOR MONSTER TROUT!
ANY LUCK?
HE HOOKED A MOOSE BUT IT BROKE OFF. I CAUGHT AND RELEASED SIX TREES AND A BAT.
COCHRAN!

"I'll release him alright . . . into a skillet!"

"It's not really a hatch. It's just Uncle Charlie's usual entourage."

WHERE ARE WE GOING, UNCLE CHARLIE?
WHERE EVER HE'S GOING!
STATE FISH HATCHERY
FISH
GAME
COCHRAN!

"It's the big one that got away."

"I TOLD you these beaver ponds were fun to fish!"

"Use your net, kid! Whatever you do, don't try to lip him!"

"When trout are feeding selectively you have to experiment 'til you find what they want, kid. Cheddar, American, Swiss . . ."

"They may be 'strike indicators' to you but they're 'bobbers' to me."

"You tie. I'll dig."

"Don't let the dog lick you in the face! He's been eating Uncle Charlie's chili!"

"Now get me a bottle of beer and we'll christen her."

"I wouldn't swim here if I was you, kid. These big browns will eat damn near anything."

WE GOT A PROBLEM, KID.
RAINBOW REDNECK
WE'VE ONLY GOT ONE CHEESE BALL LEFT...
RAINBOW REDNECK
...AND IT'S PLUGGING THE HOLE IN THE BOAT.
RAINBOW REDNECK
COCHRAN!

IT'S TIME FOR OUR SHORE LUNCH, KID.
BUT IT'S ONLY 10 O'CLOCK.
RAINBOW REDNECK
I KNOW. BUT I SHORE AM HUNGRY!
RAINBOW REDNECK
COCHRAN!

"What do you think I ought to call my cookbook, kid? 'Cooking with Duct Tape' or 'Hot Sauce and You'?"

"Uncle Charlie's making progress. He's using barbless treble hooks."

GOOD FIGHT, BIG GUY!
NOW TAKE OFF, BACK TO YOUR WATERY HOME...
...WHERE YOU'LL LIVE TO FRUSTRATE SOME POOR SONOFA BITCH LIKE ME AGAIN!
COCHRAN!

GIVE THIS GUY WHAT EVER HE WANTS, ON US!
WHAT'S THE OCCASION? JUST MARRIED? PROMOTED? DIVORCED?
HELL, NO! HE JUST RELEASED HIS FIRST TROUT!
COCHRAN!

"Another good thing about fishing with you, Uncle Charlie—when we're hungry we can eat our bait."

"The food's not so great in here but you can't beat the atmosphere."

"Do you have a HEAVY smoking section?"

"We're out of biscuits. How about a hockey puck?"

"Anybody who can still fish after eating all that is one hell of a fisherman!"

"Your usual recipe? I'll see if the cat box is clean."

"You stayed at Uncle Charlie's too long again!"

"As near as I can tell they're feeding on filter tip cigarette butts."

"Do you realize we've got enough deer hair between us to tie 157 trillion humpies?"

"Don't interrupt me! I'm reading the river and you'll make me lose my place!"

"That's one way to get a drag-free float."

"This stream has always been known for its big mayfly hatches."

"This is the only embarrassing thing about having a fly-tyer for a father!"

"Tell us about some of your experiences, grandad!"

IF I WADE OUT A LITTLE FARTHER I CAN CAST TO WHERE THOSE TROUT ARE RISING.
JUST A LITTLE FARTHER.
PERFECT!
COCHRAN!

"Sure! I know who John Quincy Adams was! I fish with his flys!"

"I TOLD you to watch your back cast!"

"Hey, this is better than a purse! One pocket for lipstick, one for credit cards, another for perfume . . . one for nail polish . . . car keys . . ."

"Your guide will be a little late. His mom is having trouble getting his waders on him."

"$300 for a day's float. $50 more if you want it video-taped, in which case choreography and custom editing will run you a little extra. And of course there's make up, script-writing, costuming . . ."

"If I'm going to video-tape this trip you'll have to lose that tacky flannel shirt and wear something trendy."

"Eeny, meeny, miney, mo? What happened to matching the hatch?"

"I'll paddle the boat but don't ask me which one of those little feathery doo-dads to use."

"You're wasting your time using anything bigger than size 20."

"They say there are some big trout in this river. If anyone ever catches one we'll know for sure."

"Quick! Work him around to this side so my logo will show."

"After you revive that six pounder he caught you can revive HIM."

YOU SHOULD'VE BEEN HERE LAST WEEK.
TROUT WERE REALLY HITTING, HUH?
NO, BUT TWO BLONDS IN BIKINIS WERE SUNBATHING ON THAT GRAVEL BAR.
COCHRAN!

WHERE THE TROUT LIE
WHERE THE TROUT FISHERMEN LIE
...WEIGHED AT LEAST 5 POUNDS!
...IT WAS A PERFECT CAST...
...PROBABLY CAUGHT 20 IN AN HOUR!
...36 INCHES!
...HE WAS THIS LONG!
...10 LBS!
COCHRAN!

"Go to the big rock, then cut toward shore and I'll hit you with a #14 Adams."

WITH THESE NEW POLAROID GLASSES I CAN SEE INTO THE WATER.
I CAN SPOT BIG TROUT AND CAST TO THEM.
LIKE THAT TEN POUNDER OVER THERE, FOR INSTANCE.

I'LL JUST DROP THIS FLY RIGHT ON HIS NOSE AND...
YES!
HMMMM... I GUESS THESE GLASSES ALSO MAGNIFY.
COCHRAN!

"Just one more cast and I'll quit for the year!"